CW00493792

BRADLEY COMPANY

Hans Halberstadt

The Crowood Press

First published in 2001 by
The Crowood Press Ltd
Ramsbury, Marlborough, Wiltshire SN8 2HR

British Library Cataloguing-in-Publication Data
A catalogue record for this book is available
from the British Library

ISBN 1 86126 425 9

Edited by Martin Windrow
Designed by Tony Stocks/Compendium
Printed and bound by Craft Print International, Singapore

Dedication:
For LTC Ricardo Riera, Commanding Officer, 2nd Battalion,
8th Infantry, 4th Infantry Division ('First At Normandy').

Acknowledgments:
I am extremely grateful for the accurate and effective supporting fires
of CPT Pete Fedak, CPT Reggie Salazar, 1LT Stefan Lockton, CPT
Acord, and all the men of 2/8 for their help and hospitality; in particu-
lar, from the ranks: SFC Ken Varnes, SFC Gregory K.Westbrook, SSG
Eric G.Garza, SSG Scot L.Thompson, SSG Edwards, SGT Israel
Montez, SSG Christopher Domont, PFC William Oliver, PFC
Carpenter, and PV2 Lawren Slockish.
    To Mr.Cecil Green, LTC Archie Davis, and MAJ Marvin Brokke
from the Public Affairs shops at Fort Hood's III Corps and 4th Infantry
Division, for their very high level of professionalism, enthusiasm, trust,
and timely help.
    To legendary and notorious armor author, the guy who knows more
about everything with tracks and wheels than I do - Michael Green, for
his archival photos and sage advice; and finally,
    To SGT Michael Pintagro and the PAO shop at NTC for yet another
lovely long vacation in the Valley of Death, the place where the men,
the machines and the doctrine all come together.

Contents

1: Genesis - A Ride, or a Weapon System?

Thirty years ago, during the coldest years of the Cold War, NATO planners had a very difficult problem. The prospect of a catastrophic shooting war with the forces of the Warsaw Pact was a serious possibility. Facing NATO forces were the vaunted 'Red hordes', the combined armies of the Soviet Union, Poland, the German Democratic Republic, Hungary, Czechoslovakia and other nations, all poised to launch a co-ordinated combined arms attack across the German plains and deep into Western Europe.

These Warsaw Pact forces were immense, extremely well equipped and trained to a high state of readiness. Their equipment was sturdy, reliable, efficient, and designed with many brilliant features based on combat experience. If the Cold War turned hot, NATO forces would face a swarm of rugged, hard-hitting T-55, T-62, and T-72 tanks supported by even greater swarms of accompanying BMP personnel carriers and supporting vehicles, hammering at NATO's thin blue line of mostly American M60 tanks and supporting infantry in their ubiquitous M113 armored personnel carriers.

Unable to match the Soviet forces tank for tank and man for man, the NATO planners developed an alternate battle concept: use smaller numbers of tanks such as the American Abrams, German Leopard, and British Challenger, each with advanced-technology weapons, extremely effective composite armor, and target detection systems that could see through smoke, rain, and the darkest night. The idea was that each of these tanks would be considerably more lethal than the Warsaw Pact systems

which they would face; and that each crew would be able to destroy several – perhaps many – enemy tanks before succumbing to the inevitable attrition of war and being killed in their turn.

The US Army's M1 Abrams tank (see EM No.28, *Abrams Company*) triumphantly proved that the concept of 'fewer but better' was viable. Despite some teething troubles and vocal critics, it turned out to be just what NATO planners had intended - 'survivable' against almost any weapon on the battlefield, incredibly lethal with its 105mm and later 120mm gun, fast, agile, and able to detect and engage targets under conditions previously believed to be impossible.

However, the 1973 Yom Kippur War between Israel and the Arab states provided the world's armies with a sobering reminder of the absolute necessity of infantry support for armor. During the first days of that brief war, Israel's highly trained and well equipped tank units on the Suez front were chopped to pieces by Egyptian infantrymen using Russian 'Sagger' wire-guided missiles from well-positioned ambushes. The Israelis had tried to use their tank units 'pure', i.e. without supporting infantry to slow them down - a fatal error, and a costly lesson.

At the time, and for many years afterwards, infantry from many nations rode to battle in the M113 armored personnel carrier (APC), a simple, reliable vehicle with half-inch aluminum armor. The M113 was and still is the classic 'battle taxi', a tracked metal box which putters around the battlefield in dozens of variants - infantry transport, ambulance, mortar platform, TOW missile plat-

form, and all sorts of other versions. There were two critical problems with the M113, however: it was much slower than the Abrams, and it was vulnerable to almost any weapon on the battlefield, from a .50cal heavy machine gun upwards.

On top of all this, beginning in 1967 the Soviets had introduced an excellent new-generation carrier, the BMP - an extremely low, fast, 'infantry fighting vehicle' with seating for ten infantrymen, a 73mm gun in a low turret, and the amphibious capability to swim rivers with ease. The BMP was no simple battle taxi that delivered its load of troops to a disembarkation point close to the fighting; it was a potent threat to every light-skinned truck and APC in range - particularly the M113s and their precious cargo of infantry.

All these factors were the inspiration for the Bradley. This was to be a new kind of combat vehicle for US and NATO forces, offering a threat to the BMP and the hordes of second-echelon combat and support vehicles on the nightmare battlefield imagined by all the antagonists of the Cold War.

Today's Bradley is the result of a long breeding program that started way back in the 1960s, if not before. Consideration of the requirement resulted in a Mechanized Infantry Fighting Vehicle concept called the MICV-65. Artist's renditions of the proposed vehicle look very much like a slightly bloated BMP. Ten years of development saw the evolution of the first really recognizable

(Above) This is a genuine Soviet BMP-2, with 30mm cannon - one of several 'threat' vehicles used at the National Training Center. The BMPs are highly regarded by the US crews who man them; this one had just helped overrun the 2nd Infantry Division's Tactical Operations Center, far to the rear of the main battle area, during an exercise.

(Opposite top) The XM723 prototype, forerunner of the Bradley series; note the small size of the one-man turret, redesigned to accomodate two men in the production vehicles. The history of armored warfare has often demonstrated the unwisdom of overloading one

man with the tasks of gunner or loader in addition to commanding the vehicle.

(Opposite) Earlier model Bradleys had firing ports in the sides of the rear compartment - note these 'ball-joints' - to allow the embarked infantry to lay down suppressive (though only approximately aimed) fire on the move. It was believed that this was good for morale, while adding to the protection against infantry anti-armor teams. There was no room to wield the standard M16 rifle inside the M2, so a buttless 'sawn off' version - the M231 Firing Port Weapon - was also provided for each man.

ancestor to today's Bradley, the XM723. The development contract for the vehicle was won by FMC (Food Machinery Corporation) in 1972, and the first prototype was delivered two years later. The XM723 shows a strong resemblance to today's M2A3, but that early version had a small, one-man turret mounting only a 20mm cannon plus a 7.62mm co-axial machine gun.

That turret, of course, has been expanded, and much of the technology of the vehicle has been enhanced and embellished. Extra kits of 'reactive' and steel armor have

been tested; better optics and weapons systems, and the latest target acquisition and fire control technologies have been added; but the basic foundations of the Bradley haven't really changed since then.

The Bradley mission

The basic mission of the Bradley is to transport infantry to critical areas on the battlefield with speed and in reasonable safety, while clearing the enemy from buildings, ravines, trench lines, and similar threat areas that cannot be countered effectively by armor alone, thus allowing the Abrams main battle tank to move safely up to the close fight. Another task is attacking secondary enemy threats such as BMPs and emplaced anti-armor teams with its 25mm chain gun and 7.62mm machine gun, freeing up the Abrams to deal with the enemy's heavy armor. The third basic mission for the Bradley is to replace the M113 as a scout vehicle, able to prowl around the flanks and forward, sniffing out enemy positions or routes of movement. The 'cavalry' scout and infantry roles employ the same basic chassis and weapons, and both vehicles carry infantry, but each has its own dedicated and specialized variant.

M2A3 Bradley Infantry Fighting Vehicle (IFV)

The M2A3 variant is the most advanced current version of the Bradley, of which the basic version has now been in service for 20 years; it is a highly capable evolution of what has proved to be a sturdy, reliable vehicle. As with previous versions, the A3 can deliver seven infantrymen wherever they are needed, protected by armor and by three excellent weapons: the M242 25mm Bushmaster

(Opposite top & bottom) In the 1970s, following the heavy Israeli tank losses to man-portable anti-armor weapons during the Yom Kippur War, several armies experimented with so-called 'reactive armor': blocks of explosive attached over the outside of AFV hulls and turrets, to detonate at the millisecond of impact of an ATGW and thus to destroy it before it could penetrate the main armor. This system had obvious disadvantages - particularly for nearby friendly personnel - and

was discarded by the US forces after extensive testing. This M3A2 is photographed both with and without plastic cover sheets over the blocks of reactive armor. (Photos courtesy Michael Green)

(Above) Despite the weight penalty, 'kits' of extra external armor plates were widely added to Coalition tanks and APCs for Operation 'Desert Storm' in 1990-91. Since the Gulf War many have been retained, like the set on this M2A2.

chain gun, the TOW (Tube-launched, Optically-tracked, Wire-guided) missile, and the 7.62mm co-axial M240 machine gun. With these three weapons systems, the Bradley can engage and defeat enemy armor, vehicles, emplacements, and dismounted infantry. In the earlier models firing ports also allowed the infantry to shoot from under cover of the vehicle's armor prior to dropping the ramp.

M3A3 Bradley Cavalry Fighting Vehicle (CFV)

The M3 series Bradley is the cavalry scout vehicle for the armored force, but only carries two 'dismounts' – infantry soldiers. The room saved is used for accomodating additional radios, ammunition, and stowage for anti-tank TOW, Dragon or Javelin missile rounds. Externally, the M2 and M3 appear identical except for the firing ports - only two were fitted to the M3A2 and none to the other cavalry versions.

BRADLEY VEHICLE CHARACTERISTICS

	M2	M3	M2A2/ODS	M3A2/ODS	M2A3	M3A3
Weight (combat, lbs.)	50,259	49,945 66,401	63,982/	64,204	66,000	66,000
Ground pressure	7.7	7.7	9.5	9.5	9.9	9.9
Power to weight ratio	20.62	20.62	18.9	18.9	–	–
Fuel capacity	175gal	175	175	175	175	175
Range	300 mi 483 km	300 mi 483 km	265 mi 441 km	265 mi 441 km	250 mi 402 km	250 mi 02 km
Speed, land (mph/kph)	41/66	41/66	38/61	38/61	35/56	35/56
Slope climb	60%	60%	60%	60%	–	–
Trench crossing	8'4"	8'4"	8'4"	8'4"	–	–
Vertical wall climb	36"	36"	36"	36"	30"	30"
Crew	3	3	3	3	3	3
Infantry capacity	6-7	2	6-7	2	7	7
Firing ports	6	0	2	2	0	2
TOW rounds (ready/stowed)	2/5	2/10	2/5	2/10	2/5	2/10
25mm ammo (ready)	300	300	300	300	300	300
(stowed)	600	1,200 600	1,200	600	1,200	
M240C co-ax (ready)	800	800	800	800	800	1,200
(stowed)	1,400	3,600	1,400	3,400	2,200	3,400
M231 FPW 5.56mm ammo stowed	4,200	0	2,200	3,400	0	0
M16 5.56mm ammo stowed	2,550	1,680	2,520	1,680	2,520	1,680

2: 'The Wiring Diagram' - Unit Organization

The Bradley company, like many combat organizations, has two personalities. The first is its administrative structure and organization, the way it looks on parade and in garrison. The second is radically different - the way it is organized in combat.

In garrison, the typical **mechanized infantry company** has four platoons (1st, 2nd, 3rd, and Headquarters) including 14 M2A3 Bradley fighting vehicles, one M113 'track', a pair of 5-ton cargo trucks, and two HMMWVs. The three numbered platoons, each with four IFVs, are the hard core of the company and the basic building-blocks of combat formations. The headquarters platoon supports the administration for the company, particularly for its commander (CO) and executive officer (XO).

Three Bradley companies form the foundation for a **mechanized infantry battalion**. The battalion adds its own **headquarters company**; this is a large and complex organization with a tactical operations center (TOC) which supports the commander and his staff with planning and co-ordination of the battalion in combat, a small command group with two Bradleys and four support vehicles, a mortar platoon, scout platoon, medical platoon with six M113 ambulances, three treatment 'tracks', and three wheeled support vehicles.

This battalion headquarters company has a small headquarters group of its own, and a logistics group to bring up the beans and bullets. All together, this mechanized infantry battalion at full strength fields 104 vehicles - 44 Bradleys, ten M113s, 26 HMMWVs, four M1064 tracks, four M577 command post tracks, four M1068 digital command post tracks, and twelve 5-ton cargo trucks.

Headquarters & Headquarters Company vehicles					
Command Group	**Staff**	**HQ Platoon**	**Scouts**	**Mortar**	**Medical**
4x HMMWV	5x HMMWV	2x HMMWV	6x HMMWV	2x HMMWV	1x HMMWV
2x M2A3	4x M1068	1x 5-ton truck		4x M1068	6x M113
	1x M113			1x M577	3x M577
	3x 5-ton truck				2x 5-ton truck

(Top) A platoon of M2A3 Bradley IFVs from 2/8th Infantry rumble up to the range after a long ride from the motor pool.

(Opposite top) LTC Ricardo Riera (left), commanding officer of 2nd Battalion, 8th Infantry with the 4th Infantry Division at Fort Hood, Texas. He is discussing with CPT Acord, one of his company commanders, the pace at which a maneuver is being carried out by the company - taking a fatherly interest, one might say.... Note that the subdued patch of the division is worn on both the left shoulder and the helmet cover; and that this infantry company commander displays Airborne and Ranger qualifications.

(Opposite) CPT Acord confers with a staff sergeant while his rifle platoons deploy from their Bradleys into a tree line. Both wear the sensor rigs of the MILES system, which registers 'hits' during simulated combat, and their weapons are fitted with both the laser projectors for this system and blank-firing devices.

(Above) SSG Christopher Domont, a platoon sergeant in 2/8th Infantry, directs his squads.

(Above right) CPL Randall, a squad leader, signals his fire teams to halt as they move through cover.

CPT Reggie Salazar on small unit tactics:

'The intent behind a "company team", whether it is mech-heavy or tank-heavy, is to have both vehicles fight together, because each brings something special to the battlefield. As a mech company commander, I will get a mech-heavy team - two mechanized infantry platoons and one armor platoon with four tanks. Those tanks bring to me that big 120mm main gun with some awesome firepower. The tanks can take the "punch in the nose" from the enemy, right off the bat. I can put those tanks forward, and since they are more survivable than my Bradleys, they can take that initial jab. When the Abrams goes up against any other vehicle, the other one is going to lose.

'Then I put my Bradleys off to the flanks and let them use their long-range TOW missile capability to take out whatever might be punching at the tanks. That's how the two vehicles really compliment each other.

'Also, the tanks are very fast - they can outrun a Bradley, so if I need to get somewhere quickly, I can send the tanks on a dash up to the objective, then bring up the Bradleys from the rear and flanks to engage at long range. The flip side of all that is that while the Bradley isn't as fast as the Abrams on open terrain, it is faster going through thick vegetation and low ground that slow down the tank - what we call "slow-go" terrain.

'I always like to fight my company "pure", with fourteen Bradleys, but when I get a chance to get some tanks, I take them. And the flip side of that, too, is that any tank company commander who gets four of my Bradleys to compliment eight of his Abrams - he can put his tanks up forward and the Bradleys off to the flanks, engaging with TOWs from long range.'

(Opposite left) SSG Varnes is the 2/8th Infantry's Master Gunner, the expert in all matters regarding the weapons systems. The patch worn on his right shoulder recalls his previous combat service with the 3rd Armored Division; and note that he wears the Combat Infantryman's Badge and Airborne wings above his left pocket.

(Opposite) A medic sets up an IV drip for a heat exhaustion casualty.

(Opposite bottom) The Army's workhorse - the 5-ton truck.

(Right) The faithful old M113 'track', still in front line service in a multitude of different roles.

(Below) CPT Peterson, an artillery Fire Support Officer, at work inside one of the M1068 command tracks of the brigade TOC.

13

3: A Walk-Around Inspection

The Bradley, like all complex weapons systems, has evolved considerably since its original configuration, and will continue to improve in the future, perhaps for many years. The remarks below are a brief introduction to today's M2A3 version.

M2A2 Bradleys at work in the scorching heat and dust of the National Training Center in the Mojave desert around Fort Irwin, California. (**Opposite**) are vehicles of the 1st Bn, 32nd Armor from the 2nd Infantry Division; that in the lower picture has the armored double launcher for the TOW missile mounted on the turret.

Hull and Drive Train

The hull and drive train for both the M2 and M3 are identical. The vehicle is just over 21 feet long, $10^{1}/_{2}$ feet wide, and almost 10 feet high. The hull is fabricated from welded 30mm aluminum armor, with spall liners inside to reduce the spray of any projectile fragments that penetrate, and brackets for add-on armor tiles on the exterior.

Power is supplied by a big Cummins VTA-903T diesel engine, delivering 600 gross horsepower (500hp in the basic M2 and M3 versions, uprated for the 'Operation 'Desert Storm' M2A2 and M3A2 versions). This powerplant displaces 903 cubic inches, and is cooled by 22 gallons of a water-based antifreeze/water mix; a 175-gallon fuel tank will keep the Bradley on the trail for about 250 miles. The engine is placed forward and just to the right of the center line of the Bradley, thus providing a bit of extra protection for the driver and some of the crew from a frontal hit.

Both the current A3 versions tip the scales at around 29 tons loaded combat weight, but can be stripped down to around 18 tons for air transport in the C-5 or C-17 aircraft.

According to the Army and manufacturer, both versions are good for 35mph on the road, but drivers report considerably higher speeds. These drivers also report that the Bradley is much faster than the Abrams tank across broken ground. That agility is on frequent display at the National Training Center, where Bradleys scream across the rocky battlefields, up and down slopes of up to 60 per cent, and across side slopes up to 40 per cent. The Bradley can climb a 30-inch wall, cross an 84-inch trench, and clear a rock on the trail 18 inches high; it can also pivot on its axis like a large, heavily-armed ballerina.

A General Electric HMPT-500-3EC hydro-mechanical transmission sends power to the 24-inch tracks, each supported by six pairs of road wheels. The tracks are sprung by torsion bars and four shock absorbers per side; the left track is slightly longer than the right, with 84 rather than 82 track shoes.

Electrical power for the Bradley's numerous systems comes from a 24-volt, 400-amp system, with starting and stand-by power supplied by six massive 12-volt, 100-amp/hour batteries.

(**Left & opposite**) Two high angles on the M2A3 of CPT Pete Fedak, commanding the Headquarters & Headquarters Company (HHC), 2/8th Infantry. In the photo at left note the heavy roof hatch of the rear compartment. This is not used for access, but when opened at a slant it gives good overhead cover for crewmen reloading from the rear of the TOW launcher, which is elevated for that purpose. The commander's hatch can also be lifted vertically rather than hinged backwards as illustrated, to allow an all-round view while giving overhead cover.

The interior arrangement of the rear compartment has been reconfigured over the years, but today the M2A3 accomodates seven infantrymen - four on the left, where the 'tunnel' beside the turret provides some extra space, and three on the right. The vehicle commander and gunner have stations in the right and left sides of the turret respectively. Thanks to their common controls either one can operate the weapons systems, allowing the other to dismount with the infantry squad if necessary.

Armament:
TOW Missile System

Under many conditions, a lightly armored infantry fighting vehicle such as the Bradley or the BMP has no business mixing it up with a main battle tank. A sabot round from a Russian T-72 would hardly slow down as it sliced through the 30mm aluminum armor of a Bradley, and the 25mm chain gun's rounds would scarcely scratch the paint on the T-72 or any similar heavily armored vehicle. But the crews of the thousands of T-72s and T-55s operated by threat nations around the world are properly wary of the Bradley - and of any other US combat vehicle equipped with the TOW missile.

A tank can engage a Bradley at about 2,500 meters; the Bradley can begin engaging the tank at almost double that range, 3,750 meters - about two miles - with a very good 'probability of kill' (PK). As long as the Bradley can outrange the enemy threat it is safe. Within the tank's engagement range, it has a real problem - but Bradley crews train to stay out of that two-klick danger area.

The TOW missile has evolved over the years into an

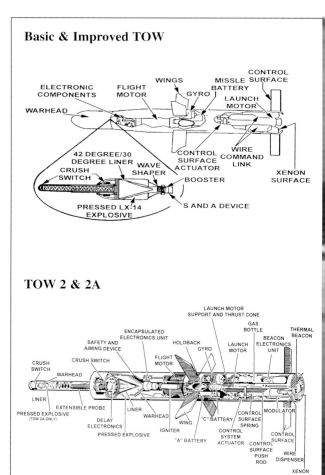

Basic & Improved TOW

TOW 2 & 2A

impressively effective weapon. It is used primarily against high-threat armor targets like enemy tanks. Most Soviet-built tanks have thick, well-shaped steel armor which is highly resistant to the tank gun projectiles of a few years ago. TOW missiles allow light vehicles like the Bradley to defeat this heavy armor without the problems of mounting a high-velocity gun; but there are a few trade-offs. The missile is much slower than a tank main gun round, so a shoot-out between the two might be one-sided. And the TOW gunner has to track the missile through his sights during its entire time of flight to the target - at least four or five seconds, and often much longer.

All variants of the Bradley currently in service carry two TOWs in the launcher, ready to fire, plus five or ten reloads, depending on model. Several types of missile are available, all of which used shaped charges to focus the effect of the warhead. The most radical of these is the new TOW-2B, a 'top-attack' weapon with a completely differ-ent kind of warhead. This senses the magnetic signature of the target vehicle as it skims just above it; then detonates twin shaped charges to form a super-high-velocity slug that punches downwards into the thin overhead armor of the target.

The TOW-2A has two warheads, the first designed to defeat enemy reactive armor before the main charge fires. This version also employs a thermal beacon that allows the gunner to track the missile through dust and smoke with better control than the earlier Basic TOW.

'The TOW is key to the Bradley's mission', says CPT Pete Fedak of the 2/8th Infantry. 'It gives me the "spank" to kill a tank before he can kill me. The perfect scenario for a Bradley commander is to use that range to your advantage. That tank can't touch me till he's within 2,500 meters. If I can pop him first, I can take him every time.

Now, the problem is, once we get within that 2,500 meters he has a direct fire weapon and can shoot at me and go hide long before I can return fire. I have to fire my TOW, track him, make sure it hits him - and the missile takes 22 seconds to get out to maximum range. That is a long time to be flapping out in the breeze in combat!'.

M240 Co-Axial Machine-gun

Enemy 'dismounts' (foot soldiers) can swarm over Bradleys, or pop up out of the woodwork with rocket-pro-pelled grenades (RPGs), rifles, machine guns, satchel charges, and all sorts of other weapons, intent on mischief. To deal with these threats the Bradley mounts a single co-axial 7.62mm machine gun on the right side of the turret, in line with the chain gun. Either the gunner or vehicle commander can operate the M240 to engage infantry.

M242 25mm Chain Gun

Although the Bradley can engage and defeat main battle tanks, its primary targets are the lighter vehicles - trucks, light armor, and particularly enemy armored personnel carriers like BMPs, which will be hunting the Bradley in return. For this kind of engagement Bradleys are equipped with a remarkable automatic cannon, the M242 'chain gun'. This weapon can also engage enemy helicopters and slow-moving fixed wing aircraft, troops in the open, and fortifications.

Several types of ammunition are available for the chain gun: an Armor Piercing Discarding Sabot round with a tracer element (APDS-T) and a depleted uranium projec-tile for use against armor; a High Explosive Incendiary projectile (HEI-T); and a very high velocity fin-stabilized APFSDS-T round designed for use against aircraft, including jet fighters.

(Opposite top) Photographed on Crittenberger Range at Fort Hood, this M2A3 shows the 'eyes' on which the 'brain' of the weapons system - the IBAS - depends for input: left, the Commander's Independent Viewer (CIV), and center, the periscope head of the gunner's Target Acquisition Subsystem (TAS).

(Above) The engine compartment of the M2A3, with the 600hp Cummins VTA-903T diesel.

(Right) The Bradley's two-foot-wide tracks give good ground pressure figures. When rigged for amphibious movement the M2 is also propelled by these tracks in water, giving a speed of around 5mph/8kmh.

(Above & opposite top) The external armor plate 'tiles' fitted to the turret and hull sides of the M2A3. Note that the latter are now manufactured with handles already attached, to make life easier for the fitters. The degree of protection afforded by these kits is, naturally, classified, but the fact that they have been retained in various forms since the Gulf War argues that they have been found effective enough to warrant the extra weight penalty.

The turret crew and driver are protected under NBC (Nuclear, Biological, Chemical) conditions by a Gas Particulate Filter Unit (GPFU); so is the rear compartment of the M3A3. The frequent need to open and close the ramp of the M2A3 made it impractical to fit a full overpressure system in the infantry version, so the embarked troops rely on their own filter units.

(Left) Detail of the headlight and driving light, and the front edge of the spaced armor plate.

(Opposite) Detail of the rear access ramp, and the small inset door - in practice, nobody uses this. The stowage bins each side of the ramp hold ammunition, rations, etc. Note also the vision blocks in the roof of the rear compartment.

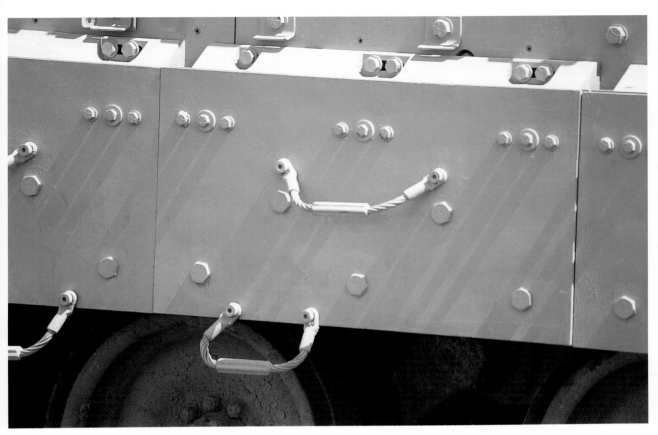

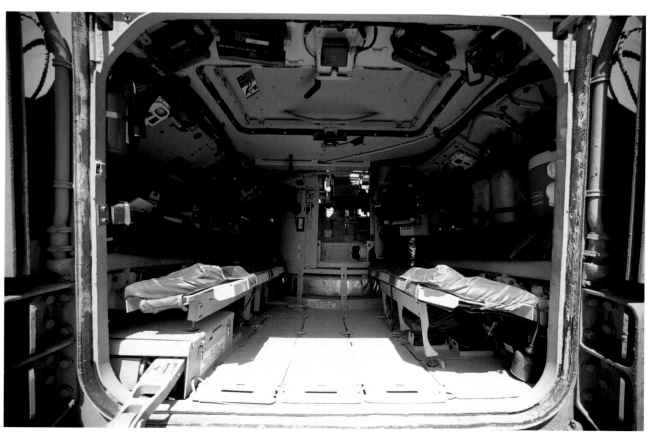

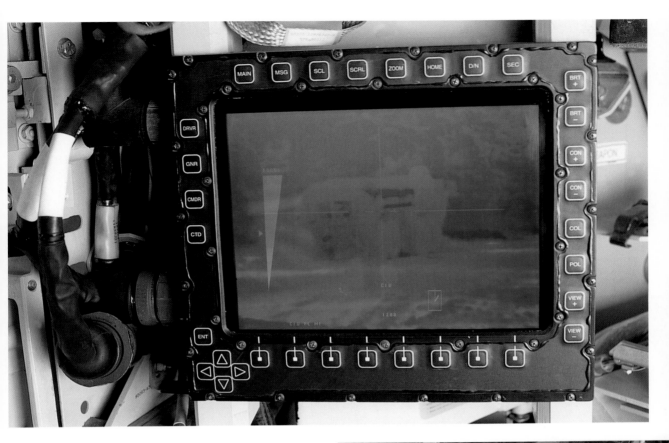

MAIN MSG SCL SCRL ZOOM HOME D/N SEC
BRT +
BRT −
DRVR
CON +
GNR
CON −
CMDR
COL
CTD
POL
VIEW +
ENT
VIEW −

(Opposite top & opposite) The infantry compartment of the M2A3 with and without its seven inhabitants. Note, opposite, the inside of the large roof hatch painted exterior sand color, contrasting with the interior pale green; and, on the right just behind the turret, the squad leader's display screen.

(Above) The display screen can show the troops several kinds of useful information when 'buttoned up'. A daylight TV picture helps orient them to the terrain around the vehicle, their objective and their route to it,

before the ramp drops. The screen can show the infra-red sight picture even when the gun is firing; the commander or gunner can zoom in on a feature to show it to the squad leader. The display can also show a tactical map with friendly and enemy positions, up-dated every few seconds. The squad leader can also use it to call for casualty evacuation, and to pass reports to higher commands.

(Right) Detail of vision block and plastic water cans in the right rear side of the troop compartment.

(Left) Detail of the Commander's Independent Viewer head, and the co-axial machine gun muzzle beside the 25mm chain gun. The three crew members wear the Combat Vehicle Crewman's helmet, but are also issued with the standard infantry 'Fritz' for dismounted action.

(Opposite) The business end of the 25mm M242 chain gun.

(Right) Ammunition for the 7.62mm M240 co-axial machine gun.

(Left) Blue identifies this 25mm HE ammunition for the chain gun as inert training rounds.

(Below left) High-velocity 25mm armor-piercing 'sabot' training ammunition for the M242 Bushmaster.

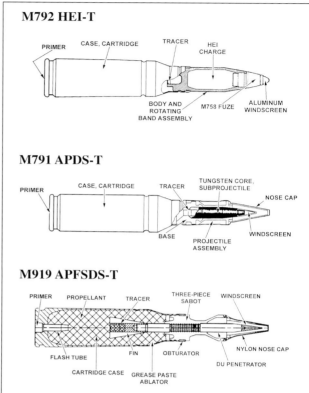

M792 HEI-T

M791 APDS-T

M919 APFSDS-T

25mm Ammunition Characteristics

	M791 APDS-T	M919 APFSDS-T	M792 HEI-T	M910 TPDS-T	M910A1(*) TPDST	M793 TP-T
Muzzle velocity	1345mps	1385mps	1100mps	1525mps	1550mps	1100mps
Time of flight:						
1,000m	0.8 sec	0.8	1.2	0.7	0.7	1.2
1,500m	1.2 sec	1.2	2.2	1.2	1.2	2.2
2,000m	1.7 sec	1.6	3.6	1.8	1.7	3.5
2,500m	2.2 sec	2.1	5.3	2.5	2.4	5.2
Case weight	458g	454g	501g	420g	420g	501g
Projectile weight	134g	96g	185g	95g	95g	182g
Tracer burn time (secs)	1.4	(**)	>3.5	>1.8	>2.4	>3.5
Tracer burn range (meters)	>2,000	(**)	>2,000	>2,000	>2,500	>2,000
Bursting radius	N/A	N/A	5m	N/A	N/A	N/A
Arming distance	N/A	N/A	10-200m	N/A	N/A	N/A
Max.effective range (meters)	2,000	(**)	3,000	2,000	2,500	2,000

Notes: * = Specifications in this column are estimated.   ** = Classified.

4: Technology in the Turret

In its original, 'plain vanilla' M2 version the Bradley was a pretty good APC - maybe not quite as good as the BMP-2, but not bad. Then the Army took some risks with the technological evolution of the vehicle, and began designing into it some very advanced systems for target acquisition, for situational awareness, and for protection. These technologies were something of a gamble, but they have mostly paid off. Today's Bradley is a combat vehicle that crews and commanders rave about - able to out-range enemy tanks, able to see the battlefield in a whole new way, and able to work closely with other combat assets like aviation and tanks.

Improved Bradley Acquisition Subsystem (IBAS)

IBAS is the acronym Bradley crews use for the system that integrates all the weapons optics and controls - the laser range-finder, gunner's periscope, second-generation FLIR (forward-looking-infra-red), day-television, turret drive, and all the electronics associated with the weapons. It is loaded with computerized technology, and it generally works like a dream.

Within the IBAS are subsystems which support the gunner and his mission: the eye-safe laser rangefinder, an automatic bore-sighting system for aligning the weapons' sights, TOW missile tracking, the viewers for the direct-view, TV, and FLIR optics, and integration with the rest of the Bradley's many systems.

The technology provides tremendous amounts of information to the gunner, commander, driver, and even to the infantry squad leader down in the troop compartment, through flat panel LED displays. These flat panel displays can show, at the push of a button, a digitized map showing the position of the Bradley and both friendly and hostile vehicles nearby - or it can show the image viewed by the commander or gunner, helping orient the infantry squad before they leave the vehicle to execute a dismounted mission – vital in those first exposed seconds.

Laser Target Acquisition Subsystem (LTAS)

One of the major components of the IBAS is the LTAS, the gunner's sights and weapon-tracking controls. The gunner uses the LTAS to identify and engage targets, day or night. His sensor systems are basically independent from the commander's systems, the CIV (see below), but integrated with them when desired by the commander.

Targets are viewed and tracked with the periscope head (P-head) mounted on the turret roof above the gunner's station on the left side. Ballistic doors protect the optics during road marches and are opened during tactical operations. These optics provide day-TV, direct view through a conventional telescopic sight, and FLIR. The direct optics and day-TV systems are back-ups for the FLIR.

Laser Rangefinder

Starting with the M2- and M3-A2ODS variants ('ODS' for Operation 'Desert Storm'), the Bradley's fire control system got a major up-grade with a new laser rangefinder linked into the Integrated Sight Unit (ISU). This rangefinder (officially called the Bradley Eye-Safe Laser Rangefinder, BELRF), will accurately determine distance to the target, from 200 to 9,990 meters, at the push of a button on the gunner's hand station. In the A3 that data is immediately displayed in the sight and pumped into the fire control computer; using that data and the pre-loaded

(Above) The M2A3 'buttoned up', with ballistic doors protecting the turret optics and the TOW launcher.

(Opposite top) Looking from left to right across the turret, from the gunner's station towards the commander's position. The most quickly noticeable difference from most AFV turrets is the absence of a

gun breech protruding into the turret space; the M242 is completely enclosed. The breech - see page 35 - is covered by the ventilated panel at left center, bearing two CAUTION notices.

(Opposite) The commander's station in the M2A3, with LED panel and control handgrip of his CIV system.

ballistic data for the ammunition selected (HE or AP sabot rounds), the system elevates the gun. The gunner's sight picture remains steady, the reticle laid on the target's center-of-mass.

Auto-Track

The IBAS has many features similar to those found on the head-up-display (HUD) in fighter aircraft, one of which is the auto-track facility. When a fighter pilot designates a target with the push of a button, his fire control system locks onto it, follows the target, and makes constant corrections for its engagement. That's the way it works on the A3 Bradley, too.

The auto-track feature can be used to designate and

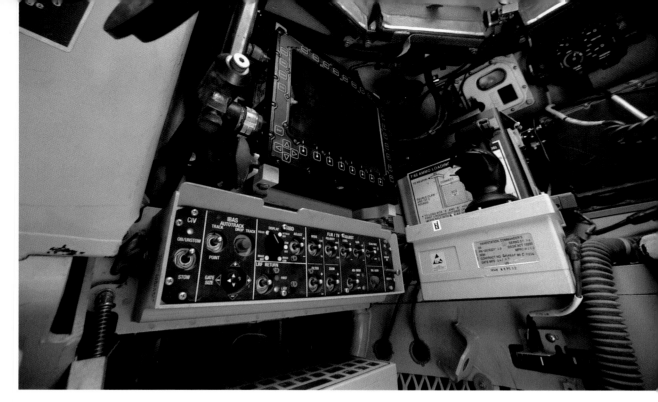

(Above) Close-up of the commander's control panel and display.

(Left) Commander's hand controller with shielded trigger.

(Opposite top) The 'P-head' of the gunner's TAS, with ballistic doors open.

(Opposite) The intercom control box at the rear of the turret.

engage one or two targets at the same time, and is intended for 'movers'. It will keep the turret oriented on the tracked target and allow for semi-automatic engagements. It seems to have particular utility for TOW engagements, with their long time of flight, and it can keep an electronic eye on a secondary target while a primary one is being engaged.

The auto-track system uses the FLIR optics, even when the gunner or commander is using the day-TV system for the engagement, and that gives it some little quirks. It will sometimes bounce from its intended target to a 'ghost target' like a tree, rock, or other terrain feature. It takes a little extra time to set up, too - and during gunnery evaluations extra time is scarce, so A3 crews haven't used it much. As one of them reports, 'theoretically, if you put a track box on a tank, when you fire a TOW, the missile is supposed to hit center-of-mass. But in gunnery we don't really use them. They aren't very fast, and they can jump onto ghost images.

'The way we expect to use them is out in the desert at a place like NTC, where you can see the enemy coming from ten klicks away and you can't even engage him till he gets to under four klicks. You can put a track box on him and follow him in to the maximum engagement line,

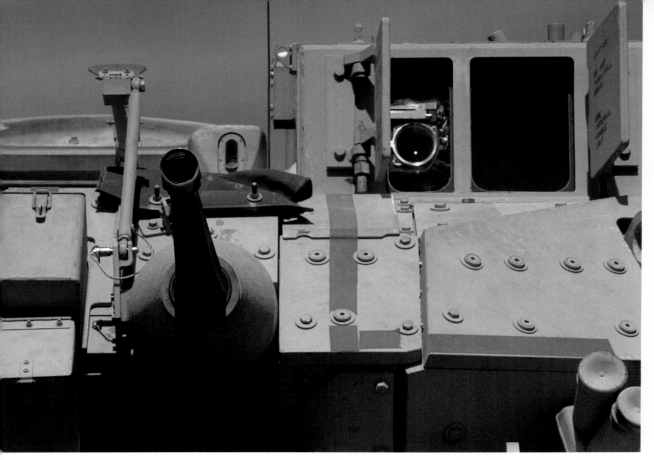

and then fire conventionally. But how often do you get that kind of opportunity? It might be a good item in the real world, but we don't know yet'.

Commander's Independent Viewer (CIV)

One of the most impressive additions to the A3, and a radical improvement in the technology of armor, is the concept of an independent viewer for the vehicle commander. Both the Abrams and Bradley are getting such a system, and it is transforming the way the armor team fights.

The CIV is a kind of electronic periscope with fully stabilized infra-red and daylight optics. Before the introduction of the CIV, the commander and the gunner were in competition for the use of the target acquisition system - one or the other could use it at any moment, but not both simultaneously. Since the vision from inside a buttoned-up AFV is very poor without this system, if the gunner was engaging a target the commander had to either watch the gunner's sight picture, peer through dim, grimy vision blocks - or stick his head out of the turret, risking hostile fire.

The CIV is mounted on the right side of the turret roof, rotates 360 degrees, and works just like the superb set of optics available to the gunner. This lets the commander search for new targets and designate them while the gunner is busy taking care of previous ones. The crews call this a 'hunter/killer' team, with the commander doing the hunting and the gunner killing the targets. By comparison with earlier engagement techniques, it is extremely fast and efficient.

This system is even more useful than that, however. Some member of the Bradley platoon will always be on watch in the middle of the night - whether in the deserts of the Middle East, or in the Mojave at the infamous National Training Center - monitoring the radios on the company net and scanning for alien invaders. The CIV makes this surveillance chore much more efficient, since the soldier on watch doesn't need to drain battery power traversing the whole turret, but only the CIV. And the CIV's optics allow him to detect vehicle targets at up to seven kilometers under good conditions - more than four miles away.

CPT Salazar on IBAS & CIV:

'The Commander's Independent Viewer is awesome. It allows that whole hunter-killer technique on the battle-field. The CIV allows me to have a 360-degree view of the battlefield at the same time as my gunner is engaging a target. I can designate a target off in a completely different direction from the one the gunner is engaging, and then hand it off to him almost instantly as soon as he's done with the first target.

'The IBAS and improved optics allow you to see much

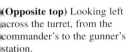

(Opposite top) Looking left across the turret, from the commander's to the gunner's station.

(Above & above right) The gunner's left and right side hand controllers, respectively. The use of these controls is explained in Chapter 7.

further down the terrain than with the A2. You can pick up a target so far away that the other guy doesn't have a clue that you're looking at him. Then you can zoom in on him close enough to tell what brand of cigarette he's smoking.

On the digital battlefield:

'Once we master the use of the "digital battlefield" technologies, we will become twice as lethal as we are today. The digital systems will radically improve our situational awareness. They will allow a commander like me to look at a map on a screen, and see where all my assets and all the enemy assets are - let's face it, when you're buttoned up in the turret, particularly in an NBC environment, you are challenged to command and control with what you can see through the CIV and the direct-view optics. It's a difficult business to figure out who's friendly and who's not, and even among other Bradleys in view, which one is your wingman and which is your platoon leader. But with the digital maps, you will be able to look at a map on the screen and see icons showing the whole situation. That's going to be great'.

Plugger

Navigating an armored vehicle has always been a major problem. Traditionally, a commander had the choice of standing in the hatch, exposed to hostile fire from all directions, or hiding out inside the turret where he was safe but somewhat blind. If he stood in the hatch, he had an excellent view of the surrounding terrain, friendly forces, plus ground and aerial threats, and could give maneuver commands to the driver based on his 360-degree view of the battlefield - until he got bushwhacked by a sniper or wiped out by an artillery airburst.

The solution to this part of the situational awareness problem is the Precision Lightweight Global Positioning System Receiver/Digital Compass System. This is officially designated PLGR in the manuals, but actually everybody calls it the 'plugger'. This is yet another digital technology, which integrates GPS (the global positioning system network of overhead satellites) and other technologies with the vehicle's multi-function display. The PLGR gives the commander extremely accurate, three-dimensional information about exactly where the Bradley is at all times, including elevation, longitude and latitude, and grid location consistent with military maps. In addition the PLGR displays the direction of travel, and can be programmed - like an aircraft's navigation system - from one way-point to another. 'Steer to' commands are displayed for both commander and driver, vastly improv- 33

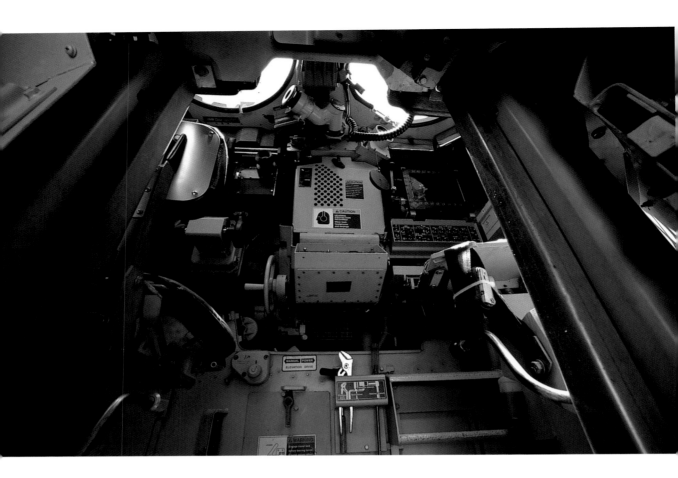

ing the ability of a small unit commander to find his way around the battlefield without blundering into trouble.

Battlefield Combat Identification System (BCIS)

Combat aircraft have used for years a coded transponder 'identification-friend-or-foe' (IFF) system to help sort out the good guys from the enemy; and soon ground combat vehicles will be getting them as well. During Operation 'Desert Storm' in 1991 a large proportion of Coalition force casualties were caused by 'friendly fire' from ground and air. To avoid a repetition of these tragic losses, the Bradley will have a Battlefield Combat Identification System (BCIS) installed when it is prepared to deploy to a combat zone.

The system allows the Bradley crew to interrogate suspected enemy vehicles with a device that transmits a millimeter wave signal; friendly vehicles will have a BCIS transponder that replies to the interrogation with a visual and audible signal. The system doesn't tell a crew that a suspected vehicle is an enemy target, and just because a vehicle doesn't return a signal confirming that it is friendly doesn't mean it can be engaged. But the BCIS will certainly help cut down on fratricidal 'blue on blue' incidents in future combat operations.

(Above) The view forwards and upwards into the turret from the rear compartment: gunner's station on the left, commander's on the right.

(Opposite top) The M2A3's weapons control panel, situated between the gunner and commander and accessible to both. Note at bottom left the selectors for the 25mm ammunition type, and high or low rate of fire.

(Opposite) With the cover above the weapons control panel hinged out of the way the rear of the M242 gun is revealed. The 25mm Bushmaster chain gun selects either HE or AP ammunition automatically on command from the gunner or commander. This makes for a somewhat complex loading sequence, for which the indicator on the rear of the cannon is essential.

Laser Warning System

Although not currently installed, the Laser Warning System will let the Bradley crew know when they are being 'lased' - a good time to go hide, or start shooting at the source of the laser, since that normally indicates that the vehicle is being engaged.

Missile Countermeasure Device (MCD)

Another battlefield system that won't be installed until Bradleys are prepared for real-world combat deployment is the Missile Countermeasure Device (MCD). This will help spoof thermal-guided missiles, but is not used in current training.

5: The Infantry Part of Mechanized Infantry

The Bradley IFV is only half of mech infantry; the other half is the 'Eleven Mikes' who ride in the back. At some point they are always going to have to get out and do their share of the assigned mission on foot, with rifles, automatic weapons, and their own anti-armor missiles.

Each Bradley platoon is organized around the 'three-by-nine' format - three men crew each vehicle, and three nine-man infantry squads make up the platoon. However, the Bradley won't carry a full squad of combat-equipped infantrymen, so these three squads are split up and carried in four Bradleys.

Each of the three squads is set up according to the classic pattern: two four-man fire teams, each with a team leader, and with a squad leader to command the whole little unit. The fire team idea is an old and effective one, the foundation for American infantry tactics. In combat one fire team sets up a 'base of fire' and beats up the enemy, keeping them scared and distracted, while the other team maneuvers in comparative (!) safety to a new position. They hit the dirt, then take over the responsibility for maintaining the base of fire. As soon as they start putting some hurt on the enemy position, the roles reverse and the first team gets up and dashes forward (usually) to a new

position, where they flop down and begin to pop away again. The process is called 'bounding'; it first appeared during World War I, when the infantry platoon acquired for the first time in history its own support weapon, and thus the firepower to make it feasible. It still works, for infantrymen of all nations and for units of all sizes - as well as for tanks and other combat units.

Bradley Infantry Fire Team

These fire teams of four men are the basic building block of dismounted operations. The fire team leader is one of two men who carry M-16A2 rifles - the same basic design that's been in the inventory since the middle 1960s, but with some improvements and enhancements. It is a lightweight, accurate, reliable weapon, firing a little 5.56mm bullet at very high velocity. With the M16A2 a trained soldier can reliably kill an enemy under typical combat conditions at up to about 300 meters - if the enemy co-operates with the process and lets the rifleman get off an aimed shot at him.

All dressed up with somewhere to go... Everybody waits for the commands 'Raise ramp!'; then, 'Driver - Move out!'.

One of the other men carries the fire team's M249 Squad Automatic Weapon (SAW). Based on the Belgian FN Minimi light machine gun, the SAW fires the same .5.56mm NATO cartridge as the M16, but in linked belts typically carried in plastic 'assault packs' (or occasionally as loose rounds in the same magazine as used in the rifle). The SAW will put 85 rounds down range each minute during sustained engagements - anything faster risks burning out the barrel and 'cooking off' chambered rounds.

The fire team is rounded out by a grenadier armed with an M16A2 to which has been attached an M203 40mm grenade-launcher. These 40mm grenades give the team a small indirect fire capability. They aren't very deadly, with a casualty radius of only about five meters, but that's enough for coping with enemy soldiers in fortified positions, in buildings, or grouped in the open. Pop one of these in the aperture of a machine gun emplacement or the window of a building where a sniper is hiding, and your tactical situation is likely to improve quickly.

All seven men on the team have PVS-7B night vision goggles (NVG) that can easily be clipped to brackets on the helmet, and the SAW gunners have PVS-4 night vision scopes. These night vision devices have helped transform the effectiveness of infantry during the past several decades, allowing operations at almost the same intensity as during daylight.

(**Opposite top**) A fire team from the 2/8th Infantry 'un-asses' an M2A3 and take up initial positions before moving out toward their objectives.

(**Opposite**) Members of a fire team moving fast. Their M16A2 rifles do not have blank firing devices, and do have the PAQ-4 laser aiming device mounted.

(**Above**) The fire teams take up security positions in case of counter-attack; soon, on the order, they will move out to assembly areas.

(**Right**) SGT Clyde Andrade of 2/8th Infantry. Squad leaders are usually sergeants or corporals, depending upon availability.

All members of the team also use a nifty little laser aiming device, the PAQ-4, which works with the NVG. This little pointer is aligned with the bore of the soldier's weapon and actuated by a small pressure switch on the M-16 or SAW stock. Its output is invisible without NVG, but shows up clearly when wearing the goggles. Put the dot on the target - an enemy soldier's center of mass - and the bullet will strike the center of the dot at normal engagement range.

Theoretically, the Bradley platoon leader has three squads assigned to him; but in the real peacetime world he is more likely to have only two - 18 instead of 27 men. That's enough to accomplish some small but important missions: clearing a small fortified position or trench, cleaning out enemy overwatch elements guarding an anti-armor obstacle, and chasing away or capturing enemy

possible so they could dismount, maneuver, and destroy the enemy without having to walk ten kilometers first. What we do real well with the infantry now is to clear terrain before sending the Bradleys into places where they might be vulnerable to enemy 'dismounts'.

'That happens when we come up on "inter-visibility lines" or IV lines as we call them - places where you don't know for sure what's on the other side, and where you might expose yourself if you creep forward for a look. We have to be real careful that way with the Bradley - its silhouette is higher than the old model, and you can easily give away your position by being a bit too far forward. So we dismount the infantry and let them clear the IV line. Then we move up and let them remount, and keep on going.

'Another use for the infantry is as anti-armor teams. All of our infantry carry Dragons, and it is a very lethal weapon system. The most dangerous thing on the battlefield is a foot soldier with a Dragon - he can take out just about anything at close or long range. If you have several guys running around the battlefield with Dragons, whether you're a tank or IFV, you'd better watch out - they're

scouts. Two squads and four fire teams can clear buildings, if they have a lot of time and fire support from the Bradleys. But perhaps the most useful thing these two or three squads can do is protect the armor from enemy anti-armor infantry teams, and to execute anti-armor missions themselves against enemy armor. As CPT Fedak says, the most dangerous weapon on the battlefield is the infantry soldier armed with Dragons and Javelins and the skills to employ them effectively.

Dragons and Javelins

For many years the dismounted infantryman has been a potent threat on the battlefield, particularly when he's armed with a powerful, man-portable anti-armor missile like the Russian 'Sagger' used so effectively by the Egyptians against the Israelis in 1973. One of NATO's answers to the 'Sagger' is the Dragon, a wire-guided weapon that is supposed to be able to defeat tanks and infantry fighting vehicles like the BMP - and it will, too, if you get a lucky grill-door shot from the rear. But the chances of killing these threats with the first shot out of a Dragon are not high - 35 per cent for a kill on a BMP-type vehicle, and only ten per cent for a first-round kill on a tank.

That situation has improved with the new Javelin, which has a laser designator instead of wire guidance - Javelins have been scoring 98 per cent kills in training. The Javelin is a 'fire-and-forget' weapon: once its infrared seeker/tracker has locked onto a target and the 127mm rocket has been launched, it will zoom off down range, maneuvering itself all the way to the enemy vehicle without further attention. It can engage targets to 2,500 meters.

CPT Salazar on the Bradley's Infantry:

'When the Bradley was designed a long time ago, its purpose was to get the infantry as close to the objective as

going to get you! The infantryman has the ability to use cover and concealment to move around - before you know it, he's behind that enemy armored vehicle and engaging it, and he's going to be successful.

'With these dismounts and their missiles, we can force the enemy to be fighting in two different directions - he's worried about the 25mm and co-ax in the short-range fight, and the TOW at long ranges, but, oh-by-the-way, coming around his flank are the dismounts with the Dragon and Javelin that came out of that Bradley. That is a real potent threat.'

(Opposite top & above) The M203 40mm grenade-launcher fitted to the M16A2 rifle, with HE round and ammunition bandolier. Although it appears clumsy the M203 is - with training - an extremely accurate weapon, which gives each fire team useful indirect fire support out to ranges of up to 350 yards.

(Opposite) PFC Rafael Ibarra, a grenadier with Alpha Company, 2/8th Infantry.

(Right) The platoon sergeant takes cover during a firefight with an opposing force. The 'bumps' on his helmet are the sensors for the MILES 'laser tag' system, which cuts out any argument about who got hit and who didn't during training battles.

These infantrymen from 2/8 all wear standard combat dress: the battle dress uniform (BDU) in woodland pattern camouflage with subdued insignia, and the 'Fritz' helmet and body armor of the Personal Armor System for Ground Troops (PASGT). Their web gear is as likely to include elements of the old green All-Purpose Lightweight Individual Carrying Equipment (ALICE) as the newer camouflage-finish Integrated Individual Fighting System (IIFS) vest. NBC kit is carried in the satchel on the left side or hip.

(Opposite) PV2 Lawren Stockish, left, of Charlie Company, 2/8th Infantry, is briefed by his fire team leader PFC William Oliver.

(Opposite below) PFC Carpenter cuts loose with his team's M249 SAW, fitted with a muzzle blank-firing device.

(Right) SGT Israel Montez prefers to pack an M203 rather than the standard M16A2. One huge difference between the GI of today and his father in Vietnam - let alone his grand-father in World War II - is the abundance of radio communications down to squad level.

(Below) All-round vigilance as the squad moves through wooded terrain.

43

(Opposite) Men of 2/8th Infantry fire live 'warshot' M47 Dragon missiles at old tank targets on the Fort Hood ranges. The missile and its disposable launch tube come as a single round of ammunition, which the two-man crew fit to a unit combining a bipod support and the sights, incorporating the AN/TAS-5 thermal night sight.

One of the Bradley's main missions is taking infantry anti-armor teams forward to terrain where they can hunt enemy tanks on foot with their Dragon (illustrated) and Javelin missiles. The Javelin launcher tube and round weigh 34lbs, so it is practical for one strong man to fire it from the shoulder like an old bazooka. The 127mm diameter projectile has a range of a mile and a half; once the IR seeker/tracker locks onto the target and the missile is on its way the gunner can forget it, taking cover from any enemy fire which may be attracted by the very visible 'signature' of such weapons. The Javelin finds its own way to the enemy tank; when it arrives it punches down through the relatively thin top armor, with devastating results.

(Right) Mock battles are fought at a realistic pace in demanding terrain, and heat exhaustion casualties are to be expected.

(Below) End of mission - men of Bravo Company, 2/8th Infantry in harbor, gratefully breaking out a cold one and heating some chow.

6: Driving the Bradley

Bradley drivers are critically important to the mission, in more ways than one. For starters, only the driver can open up the vehicle. His hatch is the only one that opens from outside, and, as PFC Vorm says, 'I'm the one with the key'.

With the padlock opened and latch disengaged, the massive hatch can easily be lifted thanks to powerful springs that balance its heavy weight. Step down onto the seat, and then drop down all the way and get comfortable.

Most of the controls are very similar to those of any modern car with automatic transmission, but with a few twists. There is no key, so to start it you go to the master control panel above your right knee. Switch Master Power to ON; now battery power is available to the Bradley's systems.

To start the engine, first set the Engine Accessory switch to ON, and press in on the Fuel Shut-Off button

An M2A3 driver from 2/8th Infantry shows off his unit's unofficial skull-and-crossbones helmet badge as he emerges from his place of work; and **(below)** detail of his armored hatch from the outside.

(**Left**) General view of the driver's station, looking forward from the 'tunnel' to the left of the turret.

(**Below left**) The foot pedals - brakes and accelerator.

(**Right**) Driving any armored vehicle while 'buttoned up' takes training and practice. The vision devices always give a limited field of view, and depth perception is distorted. Note the restriction of this Bradley driver's view to the right; he needs fairly constant input from the turret crew. In action, of course, they won't be out there 'eating dust', but even from their interior stations their vision devices at least give a 360-degree field.

just to the right of the main panel; this allows fuel to flow. Next, find the transmission selector on your right side; it should already be in the neutral position, so move it to the right, into START, and the engine will fire up. You don't normally need to pre-heat the cylinders, and you don't need to wait for the engine to warm up - the vehicle can be driven away immediately, if necessary. (Previous models produced large clouds of white smoke while they were warming, but the M2A3 has components that very effectively eliminate this potential visual signature.)

Unless you want a lonely drive, remember before moving to drop the rear compartment ramp. The switch is behind your head; press in and down on the control lever, and the ramp will slowly go down. The gunner and commander will come aboard, squirm up into the turret, and begin powering up their own systems.

When he's ready to move the Bradley commander (BC) will give the order 'Driver, raise ramp' - that means you. First, however, you should turn and look for a 'thumbs up' from the troops in back, verifying that it is safe to do so.

Close the driver's hatch and wait for the next command - 'Driver, move out'. Your vision through the three little bullet-resistant vision blocks is surprisingly good, once you get used to it. The periscopes are about a foot higher than eye level, and that takes some adjustment. Your view to the right is blocked somewhat by the engine, but the BC

keeps alert for hazards from that direction and will let you know if there's a problem.

Driver's Vision Enhancer (DVE)

The hatch must be closed at all times when the Bradley is being driven outside the motor pool. You haven't lived until you've tried driving a 'buttoned-up' armored vehicle along a faint tank trail in the desert, in the middle of the night, with clouds of dust obscuring the terrain - and knowing that somewhere out there is a deep gully, anti-tank ditch, and/or enemy units somewhere nearby. The commander will provide some guidance, but the driver's vision is strictly limited in such circumstances, no matter how good the vision blocks are. They inevitably get dirty and dusty, and at best provide only a narrow view of the area to the vehicle front, between about the 10 o'clock and 2 o'clock positions. Since so much of modern Army doctrine emphasizes night operations, these factors combine to make the driver's job a challenging one. That's where the DVE comes in.

The DVE is a thermal viewer that is a kind of passive 'starlight scope', offering a somewhat enhanced 'sight picture' for the driver. It provides him with a rather blurry and intermittent green and black picture of the world outside, and some drivers prefer it to the periscopes. It gives a wider field of view, and if you need to look at something

to the left or right the whole thing can be rotated for a better view. Bright lights, tracers, illumination rounds, and muzzle flashes create momentary hot spots on the viewer, making the image hard to interpret for a few seconds; and a bright image on the DVE can also inhibit the driver's own night vision.

During tactical operations, the driver is likely to get his directions from both the gunner and the BC. A platoon leader or company commander is busy with maps, radios, giving orders, and scanning for targets, so he will sometimes instruct the gunner to maneuver the Bradley.

PFC Vorm on driving the M2A3:

'A lot of where we go is up to the driver - I try to find the smoothest route so the gunner isn't being bounced around while he tries to put the reticle on target. You do that on your own, once the BC has indicated where he wants to go. But if something changes and I don't see it, the BC or gunner will call "go left" or "go right", and then I'll try to find the best path from there. In a tactical situation, you interact a lot - we are constantly talking because things are constantly changing.

'Driving the Bradley is quite exciting. It can be hot in there, and it can be tiring if you do it for a very long time, but it has always been fun for me. That's especially true when the BC says "Get us out of here!", and there are thirty tanks chasing us. Then I can take off - the thing will actually go airborne, if you let it. I have had it up to forty-two miles per hour.

'It's great to get out and maneuver, to let the machine do what it was designed to do. You have to be careful about banging the crew around, but other than that, you do what's required to accomplish the mission. I've taken it through mud, water up to my hatch, and down hillsides that seemed nearly vertical. It's a good machine!'.

(Above) The secondary systems panels to the left of the 'butterfly' yoke controlling the hydrostatic steering system: bilge pumps for use when the Bradley is prepared for amphibious movement, fire suppression, smoke generator and light switches, above the navigation system screen. Ahead of the yoke are the main engine instruments.

(Opposite top) The master control panel, with to the right the fuel shut-off and set throttle controls.

(Opposite) The automatic transmission control to the driver's right.

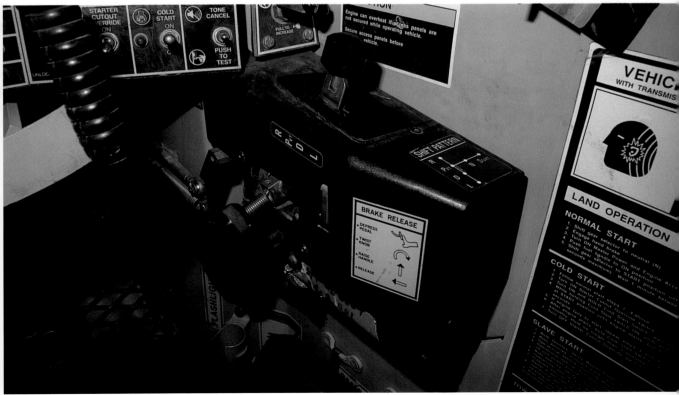

7: Into Battle - Operating the Weapons Systems

Well, now that you've been to school on the Bradley and all its basic systems, it's time to really understand how it all works. You can't fully appreciate a combat vehicle's vices and virtues unless you've tried it out yourself, preferably with bullets pinging off its armored hide. So, thanks to the magic of the printed page, we will put you in the gunner's seat for a little on-the-job instruction; and to make it complete, we will let you try everything out in combat.

Your Bradley is an M2A3 model, complete with the Combat Identification System, Missile Countermeasure System, and Laser Warning System. It is forward-deployed as part of an armored task force, in a 'mech-heavy company team supporting a secondary effort. Our unit - Alpha Company, 2nd Battalion, 8th Infantry Regiment, 4th Infantry Division (A/2-8 IN) - is deep inside Upper Slobovia. Upper Slobovia is a high desert nation whose terrain is extremely arid, rocky and mountainous (strangely resembling the landscape of the National Training Center in California...). This terrain has broad, open valleys with room for entire brigades to maneuver, surrounded by rugged hills and ridges full of hiding places for infantry scouts and anti-armor missile teams.

We'll put you in the platoon leader's vehicle, designated Alpha Two One - that's for Alpha Company, Second Platoon, Track One. You will replace the gunner, who has become a casualty. The ramp is down and the commander and driver are waiting. Enter the vehicle from the rear and then squirm into the turret. Slide into the gunner's seat on the left, and put on your Helmet, Combat Vehicle Crewman's (CVC); adjust the microphone so that it just touches your upper lip. The infantry have a job elsewhere, so straight away you hear the commander say, 'Driver - raise ramp'.

We've been briefed to prepare to defend in sector against a battalion-sized attack by elements of the Slobovian Army's 32nd Guards Motorized Rifle Regiment. According to our operational order, the Slobovians are mounting a major attack, in corps-sized strength, across a front 40 kilometers wide. The Intel weenies report that lead elements of the enemy are moving in our direction and are expected to exit Goatscrew Pass, 15 kilometers to our direct front, sometime within the next hour. There will be a battalion-sized task force with tanks, APCs, several engineering vehicles, infantry, and self-propelled artillery.

In a perfect world we would have lots of attack aviation assets overhead - A-10s, F/A-18s, and AH-64 helicopters - to start whittling down the enemy's strength as they move through the narrow valley toward us; but very few of those assets are available for us today, being concentrated on the main enemy effort 20 kilometers to the east. Our artillery support, too, is extremely limited; so we are pretty much

on our own here in our sector. Alpha Company is a mech-heavy task force - the battalion commander has 'chopped' (temporarily assigned) one platoon of M1A2 Abrams to our Alpha Company, and chopped a platoon of our Bradleys over to a tank company in return. We have two platoons of Bradleys and one of Abrams while the tank company has the reverse. The resulting mech-heavy and tank-heavy company formations will last only as long as the commander thinks they solve a problem for him; then they will evaporate in favor of some other task organization designed for a different problem. Right now he has us in well prepared fighting positions, in turret defilade, with just the CIV and P-heads exposed to direct fire.

The battlefield

We are defending a broad desert valley between two steep, rocky ridges. This valley is an avenue of approach for the enemy force; if they can punch through it, they will have a clear shot at the vulnerable support areas in the rear of the main body. Across this valley the Engineers have constructed a massive obstacle - a deep trench too wide for a tank to cross unaided, supported by lots of razor wire and mines, both anti-tank and anti-personnel, all designed to inhibit the enemy's engineers when they try to breach the obstacle. To make it even harder, both ends of the obstacle are over-watched by Alpha Company's dismounted infantry; the company commander has placed

them in the rocks with machine guns and Dragons to slow the breaching teams and perhaps kill them off.

The BC stands in the turret and you join him, standing on your seat, to get a better view. Sunrise is almost an hour away, but the sky to the east is beginning to turn purple. Soon, a tinge of red appears, then the glitter of sunlight reflected from ground attack aircraft swooping above the ground, far away.

Sunrise is 15 minutes away. Our attack aircraft are now much more visible, perhaps only 15 kilometers to the east. They dive, squirm, pop flares, release weapons, and squirm away. One pulls out, pursued by a small dot of light; the pilot pops chaff and flares, but the missile isn't spoofed. The A-10 trails fire, banks hard to the right, and you can just barely make out the pilot eject, his parachute blossoming in the first rays of the sun. Black smoke from burning vehicles rolls up from the valley; the enemy attack is slowed only momentarily, ground down very slightly, and then comes into sight. You slide down into your station, and button up your hatch.

Okay, we're ready to engage the first target. The kill zone is behind the obstacle where the enemy assault will probably stall for a few minutes while their breaching team attempts to get some lanes through the obstacle. Since this kill zone is from 3,000 to 3,500 meters away, it is ideal for our TOW missiles. We have seven of them on board, two in the launcher and five inside.

The Soviet- and Chinese-made armored fighting vehicles most likely to be fielded by 'threat' nations.

(Opposite top) The formidable T-72 main battle tank.

(Opposite) The elderly but still quite widely encountered T-55. It represents no danger to an M1 Abrams MBT, but no Bradley commander wants to get within range of its main gun.

(Above) The excellent BMP-2 infantry fighting vehicle.

Engaging with TOW

There are limits on where you can fire TOWs, and you should go through your mental checklist: back-blast area clear of personnel to 50 meters; no power lines between us and the target; no brush, trees, or antennas in the line of flight; the vehicle is on a flat surface - more than ten degrees side-slope can cause a miss.

Confirm MASTER POWER SWITCH is ON, turret in POWER mode, and the sight shield doors on the P-head are open. The Bradley has to be completely buttoned-up to launch; if it isn't the OPEN HATCH/DOOR light will go on. Verify the NO FIRE ZONE and TOW MALF lights are out. On the System Control Box, press and hold the TOW MODE button; the TOW indicator light will come on and stay on. At the same time, the viewfinder displays a little TOW missile symbol at the bottom, and it shows a TOW-2A is loaded and ready to fire. The system has been bore-sighted and the fire control system is nulled. Set the viewfinder control to FLIR and LOW MAG.

There are three enemy tanks in our sector, still well out of range but closing fast. The Slobovian formation remains in a ragged line abreast - about 70 combat vehicles, including at least 30 tanks and 20 BMPs, plus some combat support and engineering vehicles. Using the gunner's control handles by rotating to the left and tilting back at the same time, you can steer the viewfinder image onto the center of your sector.

Although the TOW can be selected in LOW MAG, you can't fire it unless HIGH has been selected; that control is a button under your left thumb. Press it, and the viewfinder cycles back and forth, from narrow field to wide. Leave it in HIGH.

'Gunner, missile, tank!', you hear the commander call. He uses his controls to shift your field of view onto his selected target. Got it? Call 'Identified', and prepare to engage. You can't shoot on your own, though - the BC is responsible for everything the vehicle does, particularly when it comes to shooting. Track the target and wait for his execution command.

In HIGH MAG, put the cross-hairs on the center of mass of your primary target, then 'box' it with a track gate. The AUTO TRACK/AUTO POINT switch is controlled by your right thumb, on the upper right side of the grip. Push it forward momentarily, and a flashing box will appear in the viewfinder along with a label in the upper left corner, TRK 1, indicating that this is your first tracked target. The box will be much larger than the target; it's 55

(**Left**) Bradley commander at his station.

(**Below**) Close-up of the M2A3's main weapons control panel.

(**Opposite**) M2A3 gunner in action.

LTC Ricardo Riera on gunnery: 'Successful gunnery involves 45 per cent technical skill, 5 per cent luck, and 50 per cent voodoo.'

default size is for a tank at 1,500 meters, so it must be resized. Another control on the same grip controls the size of the box, up or down to make it bigger or smaller, left or right to make it expand or contract laterally. Bring the box down to just fit the target. Move the AUTO TRACK switch forward again; the box stops flashing and is now solid. Your fire control system is locked onto the target and the selected weapon is almost ready to fire.

Repeat the process for your secondary target - center it, box it, adjust the box, hit AUTO TRACK again. The box goes solid; you can engage it almost immediately after the first one is destroyed. You can also move the sight around while the system continues to track both targets, searching for other opportunities and threats.

This first TOW shot will be tracked manually, so disengage the auto-tracker by releasing the palm switch. Depress the palm switch again (it's a kind of safety catch); then raise the launcher by moving the launcher switch on the weapons control panel to UP - the indicator light will confirm the launcher in position. Now you press the TOW button on the panel to select the weapon.

Arm the system by moving the switch on the weapon control panel up to the ARM position; the system is ready for launch. You've been told that we are in WEAPONS FREE condition, authorizing you to fire on any target not explicitly identified as friendly. 'Lase' the target - 3,700 meters, just within maximum range. Time to get to work. The commander orders, 'Fire'.

Using the GHS, keep the cross-hairs right on the center

of mass of the target, and track it with the reticle right where you want the missile to impact.

On the lower front of both handgrips is the 'palm switch'; squeeze it. While keeping it depressed, announce 'ON THE WAY'; pull the trigger switch on either left or right hand controller grip with your index finger - *and hold it!* The TOW system takes a second and a half to launch, a period that may seem like an eternity. This fools some inexperienced gunners into thinking that nothing has happened. If you release the trigger or palm grips now, the missile will abort - you will have wasted the shot, a lot of money, and perhaps some friendly lives.

The Slobovian tank continues to close, head on. Even

though the armor is thickest at this aspect, you have a good chance of killing it as long as you get a good hit. The rest of the process isn't complicated - no range calculation, no lead to worry about. Even from inside the buttoned-up Bradley, the noise of the TOW as it launches is loud.

The missile appears in your field of view, somewhat out of focus. It seems to bounce and bob along, flitting away in the general direction of the target. This movement is very distracting, and it looks like the weapon is going to miss, so novice gunners feel a strong urge to try to steer it back on target - a big mistake.

You must keep the palm switches depressed and continue to track the target for what seems like a week but is really only about 20 seconds. During that time the missile will seem to bob and weave down range, its little guidance motors flashing intermittently, keeping it on course. Hold the sight squarely on the target center of mass and - the TAS image momentarily blanks out from the flash and smoke of the impact... When the sight image returns, shift back to LOW MAG. Now you can see the tank turret falling back to earth like a dropped skillet, while the hull slides to a stop in a ball of fire from the burning propellant, warheads, hydraulic fluid and diesel fuel. Report to the commander, 'Target destroyed'.

Auto-tracking

'Gunner, missile, tank', the BC calls again. Now we'll take out another tank with the remaining TOW in the launcher, this time using the auto-tracker. Select MSL-2 on the SCB weapons panel to prepare the second missile for firing. This will be one of the top-attack 2B models.

Lay the cross-hairs over the next primary target, squeeze the palm switch, and press the auto-tracker switch; the target is roughly boxed with flashing lines. Adjust the top and side brackets to box the target more tightly, while still holding the palm switch down; then hit the auto-track control once more. The viewer symbology shows a solid box, and a TOW-2B icon at the bottom of the screen.

The tank is maneuvering furiously across the broken ground, but the box stays with it. Arm the missile by resetting the ARM/SAFE/RESET switch on the SCB to RESET and back to ARM. The ready light comes on. The BC gives the order, 'Fire!'.

Answer with 'On the way'. With the palm switches still depressed, squeeze the trigger and hold them while tracking the target with the GHS. After a second and a half the TOW launches. Track the target as before, but the missile will not strike center of mass. This time it flies just over the top of the Slobovian tank, above the cross-hairs, and detonates, punching a hole through the thin roof armor. The enemy vehicle comes apart at the seams.

Report to the BC, 'Target destroyed'. He responds, 'Cease tracking'.

*　　*　　*

The engagement area is already littered with wrecked and

damaged combat vehicles. The tanks go first, and as the enemy force continues to close the Abrams begin to fire when the T-72s reach their 'trigger line' at 2,500 meters. The terrain and obstacles all serve to funnel the enemy into the engagement area where they are picked off in turn. But the mass of vehicles, their speed, the kicked-up dust and the clouds of smoke they spread to obscure the battlefield all make it difficult for us to get them all, and some are forcing their way through. One breach has been made by Slobovian engineers in our sector, and they've got a bridge over the ditch in another. Slobovian air-burst artillery is keeping the heads of our infantry down at the ends of the obstacle, letting the enemy's breaching teams clear the mines and wire and bridge the trench in two more places. And they are starting to leak around the ends of the obstacle belt, too, overwhelming our force by sheer numbers and speed, skilfully deployed.

Now that the range has closed, the Abrams take out the tanks far faster than we can, and we now have other priorities - the BMPs that have crossed the obstacle and are working their way toward us. Some have already turned their dismounts loose, and the enemy infantry has disappeared into the little gullies and wadis all over the terrain in our front, safe from all direct fire weapons and able to sneak up on us. They will have to be dealt with later. It is time to crank up the chain gun.

Engaging with the 25mm gun

The M242 system has previously been bore-sighted and zeroed; both AP and HE ammunition are in the boxes, and the feeder is loaded. The turret is in POWER mode, the ARM/SAFE/RESET switch is set to SAFE. Now you must set up the Target Acquisition System.

First, check the status lights at the bottom of the panel and make sure the gun malfunction light is out. Open the cover on the rear of the gun; make sure the drive handle is engaged and locked and doesn't turn more than a half-inch. Move the manual safety handle from SAFE to FIRE; check that the bolt indicator is in SEAR, and put the cover back on. The SEAR/MISFIRE light should be on.

'Gunner, sabot, PC!', you hear the BC call on the VIC - he means that the target is a personnel carrier. He takes back control of the IBAS and your viewer image slews over to the right. Near the center of the image is a BMP roaring toward us. You find the BMP and lay the reticle on its center of mass, at the same time responding, 'Identified!'.

Quickly switch from LOW to HIGH MAGnification; press and hold the palm switches; then 'lase' the target by pushing forward the the laser rangefinder control on your left GHS grip. The range is displayed in the viewfinder, down at the bottom - but it is indicating 'multiple returns'. You have a 'bad lase'; the laser has received two readings, one from the target and another from a rock in the line of sight. Lase it again, this time on a slightly different part of the BMP - a good return this time, range 1,954 meters.

The gun controls are on the same weapons panel as those for the TOW, directly below the missile switches. The commander called for sabot, so select AP on the panel for armor-piercing fire control solutions and to feed the proper ammo into the gun. Select the firing rate; your choice is SS for single-shot, LO for 75-125 rounds per minute, or HI for 175-225rpm - set it to HI. Then arm the gun with the same ARM/SAFE/RESET switch.

'Fire!' - all you have to do now is make sure the palm switches are depressed, and squeeze the trigger. The fire control computer will make all the calculations to put the first round into the target, just as long as you put the cross-hairs on the center of mass and track the BMP smoothly.

The gun pumps out the rounds slowly enough that you can easily control the number of projectiles sent down range - one, two, three. You can see the tracers burn across the distance to the enemy APC, then burrow into it. The tracer is a bright ball cutting an almost straight line toward the BMP. Sparks fly and debris spatters from its hull, and the target vehicle slews around but doesn't stop. The crew may be dead, dying, or just getting ready to shoot back. The commander hasn't given the order to cease fire, so pump three more rounds into it - *thump, thump, thump!* More sparks, and now smoke and flame are visibly pouring from the BMP - some of the depleted uranium sabot rounds apparently punched into the fuel cells on the rear doors. Report, 'Target destroyed'.

Engaging with the 7.62mm co-ax

'Cease fire', the commander replies; then he hurriedly adds, 'Gunner, co-ax, troops!'. He slews the turret over to the right, and there they are - a squad of enemy infantry working their way toward our positions. They are using excellent movement technique, one team setting up a base of fire while the other bounds from one patch of cover to the next. The rocky terrain and dry stream beds have let them get to within about 500 meters.

'Identified!' - 'Fire!'.

You've already selected the co-axial machine gun by punching the 7.62MM switch at the bottom center of the weapons panel, and you've verified that its ready light has come on, indicating that it is now the active system. Use the laser rangefinder again while the cross-hairs are on the

general area where the enemy dismounts are maneuvering; then wait for their next bound while calling again, 'On the way'. This is a tricky engagement and hard to evaluate, so the BC will be watching the effect of your fire carefully.

In ones and twos the enemy soldiers will try to dash from one protected position to another. As they make their move across a flat, open area one of the alternating teams is exposed. Again, make sure the palm grips are down, then squeeze the trigger. Steer the cross-hairs in a Z-pattern, sweeping the beaten zone from right to left, up and across, then right to left, in a long burst.

The 7.62mm M240 machine gun will fire 650 rounds per minute if you simply hold the trigger down - but not for long. The barrel will quickly burn up if you fire long bursts. When it gets hot enough, you can't stop it: the rounds 'cook off' from the heat of the barrel. The SOP is to allow four or five seconds of cooling between each short burst, sending about 100 rounds down range each minute. Even then, the barrel has to be changed every ten minutes - and you really don't want to have to do that during combat; so keep the rate of fire down, and on target.

Some of the enemy infantry drop, dead or wounded; others seem to avoid the bullets entirely, find cover, and disappear from view. Wait to see what happens; when some of them make another rush, light them up. Continue to engage the infantry until the commander calls 'Cease fire'. When you look around, the engagement area is littered with burning vehicles and enemy soldiers with their hands in the air. End of mission.

CPT Pete Fedak on gunnery:

'The Bradley is an awesome, powerful weapons platform, and the improvements made on the A3 are great. The digital systems added, like the CIV, made a huge difference.

'When I first learned gunnery on the Bradley, you had two choices: you could stand up in the hatch and try to find targets (and I could never find them that way), and then try to get your gunner to find them by slewing the turret in that general direction; or I would get down in the turret and look through the thermal sight, and try to find them that way. So in the old A2 days the commander was just trying to help the gunner out.

'Now, with the CIV, we have a whole new tool. With the FLIR thermal viewer on the A3 we have 4-power, 12-power magnification, and it is a great way to pick up targets. You scan in low power, and when a target appears it is very noticeable. Then you zoom in for a closer look, and designate it for the gunner. The time saving on multiple engagements is phenomenal.

'The other great improvement on the A3 is the ballistic solution for the chain gun. In the old A2 days you had to guesstimate the range in a hasty engagement. During gunnery evaluation, you could cheat - they told you in advance what the target range would be, and you could dial that into the system in advance. But with the laser rangefinder you just lase the target, and the ballistic software does the rest.

'That has really changed the mindset of Bradley gunners - the old Bradley was like an "area" weapons system, like a machine gun. You used to throw a burst out there and see where it landed, then adjusted from there. These guys were good at it; but the new A3 is more like a sniper rifle - if your technique is good, your first round is on target.

'There are two hunter/killer scanning techniques for the Bradley commander and gunner. The most common is for the gunner to scan from the 9 o'clock position to about 1 o'clock, while the BC scans from 11 o'clock to 3 o'clock. The slight overlap helps prevent targets from getting lost, and this is the system favored by most BCs. The alternate method has the gunner searching from 9 to 3, but looking for near and immediate-threat targets, out to, say, 2,000 meters, while the BC also scans from 9 to 3, but looking for long-range targets from 1,000 to 4,000 meters.

'You always scan in low magnification, then zoom in to inspect hot flashes. There are always rocks or cows that show up during the scan which look like potential targets. You center the sight on it, then quickly switch to high-mag; you should be able to tell instantly if it is a target or not. And you want to have a pretty quick scan in low-mag, because the targets will really pop out at you. You search in low-mag, identify in high-mag, then come back to low-mag to see what else might be nearby.

'Here's how it works with a single enemy target vehi-

(Opposite) The 25mm chain gun firing on the ranges.

(Right) The chain gun firing at night.

(Above) Infantry 'dismounts', seen through the thermal night sight.

cle. The gunner and BC scan their sectors, and the BC picks up a hostile BMP in his scan. He quickly alerts the gunner, calls for the ammunition he wants used to engage the target, and identifies the target - say, "Gunner! Sabot! PC!". Before the A3 came along the BC also had to call out the range, but that part of the fire command is now discarded. The gunner will normally find the target without any further help, but if he calls "Cannot identify!", on an A3 the commander can put what he sees right in the gunner's sight picture. The BC calls "Target designate", and he hits the target-designate button on his commander's hand station (CHS); the gunner's field of view will quickly slew over to the azimuth of the new target. If the crew have properly aligned their optics during the bore-sighting procedure just before the operation, it should show up in the center of his display, and when he sees it he'll respond, "Identified!".

'If the gunner discovers the target first, he calls "Identified, PC!". The BC still has to look in his remote binocular display (RBD) on his IBAS and see for himself; then he gives the fire command. That's because the gunner

61

can't fire on his own, but must always wait for the vehicle commander to tell him to shoot, and tell him to cease firing. The commander orders, "Fire!".

'The gunner puts the reticle on the sight, and, if the target is a "mover," begins tracking it, all with his GHS; he lases the target at least once, evaluates the range information displayed in his sight, and if at all suspicious about it, lases again. He verifies that the proper type of ammunition is selected - his sight includes this information, along with the range, down at the bottom of the screen. When satisfied, he calls "On the way!" - that alerts the whole crew that the weapon will be firing, and by SOP the trigger is fully depressed as he says the "Y" in "way".

'If you're familiar with the A3, and have done everything right, and have a sabot round already loaded, then that first round will normally be right on target, and so will the rest. But if it has previously been firing HE rounds at a thin-skinned vehicle like a truck, one of these will still be on the chain gun's bolt face, and will have to go out the tube before the first sabot round is fired, and it will not be effective. The ballistics of the two basic types of 25mm ammunition are quite different - the HE round is much slower than the sabot - and it will fall short of the proper aim point for the AP rounds for which the ballistic computer has developed its solution. HE rounds are good to around 1,400 meters, but beyond that their trajectory makes it difficult to hit vehicles reliably. Sabot rounds

(Above) There is a famous quotation from the poet Matthew Arnold about the 'darkling plain' where 'ignorant armies clash by night'. Today's battles are mostly fought at night, and today's technology has replaced ignorance with an extraordinary degree of precise information available to soldiers far down the chain of command.

(Opposite) Classic view of an M2A2 from the 2nd Infantry Division maneuvering in the Mojave Desert.

have a flat trajectory that makes it much easier for the gunner to "spank" target vehicles out to 2,000 meters and beyond.

'The commander evaluates the effectiveness of the engagement and calls "Target destroyed, cease fire" - or if it needs more attention, he'll provide corrections and the gunner continues to pour rounds into it. The commander is always responsible for everything the vehicle does. The gunner can call "Target destroyed", but he doesn't stop firing till I call "Cease fire".

What's wrong with this picture?

The description of an engagement in the last chapter is a best-case scenario of how the weapons are supposed to be used in combat; but that isn't very often the way things go at the National Training Center. Even though the M2A2 Bradley performed very well in Operation 'Desert Storm' (known to the troops as 'The Great Drive-By Shooting'), and even though the A3 model offers great improvements, nevertheless all soldiers know that combat operations are full of systems failures, jammed weapons, defective missiles, and an unco-operative enemy.

Bradley crews and their infantry expect to receive accurate and effective return fire, and artillery air-bursts that cut TOW wires. They almost never have enough time to dig good defensive positions for all vehicles, or to fully develop battlefield obstacles. At the NTC, Bradleys do their share of 'dying'. The new A3 is going to make life tougher for the OPFOR, but their T-72s and BMPs will continue to make survival tough for armor and mech infantry units and their vehicles.

The Army puts a lot of emphasis on something the soldiers call 'lessons learned', and they have applied the lessons of NTC and the Gulf War to Bradley systems and doctrine, with impressive results. It is a great system, with great crews; but the Bradley is not bullet-proof. The main hazard of the Great Drive-By Shooting is that American soldiers may get complacent about the effectiveness of their weapons and doctrine. The T-72 wasn't the Russians' best system, and the Iraqis did not employ it to its best advantage. Next time, instead of T-72s and BMP-1s and -2s, American armor units might be facing well-handled T-90s and BMP-3s.

The BMP-3 is a very significant threat system - a 30mm gun, a 100mm gun/anti-tank missile system, and 7.62mm co-ax. The 100mm gun is stabilized and, if the auto-loader works as advertised, it will put ten rounds down range per minute. The BMP-3 doesn't seem to have the advanced digital target acquisition and situational awareness capabilities of the Bradley A3, however; and that would be a severe problem for the enemy in an engagement where everything else was equal.